NOW, SOMEHOW

poems by

Judith Terzi

Finishing Line Press
Georgetown, Kentucky

NOW, SOMEHOW

Copyright © 2022 by Judith Terzi
ISBN 978-1-64662-934-3 First Edition
All rights reserved under International and Pan-American Copyright Conventions. No part of this book may be reproduced in any manner whatsoever without written permission from the publisher, except in the case of brief quotations embodied in critical articles and reviews.

ACKNOWLEDGMENTS

I wish to thank the editors and co-editors of the following journals where these poems first appeared:

Atlanta Review: "Now, Somehow"
The Examined Life Journal: "Valentine"
Gyroscope Review: "Hard C"
L.A. Art News: Poet's Place: "Raga"
Lunch Ticket: "Transplant"
MacQueen's Quinterly: "Fire Season 2020"
Miju Poetry & Poetics, Korean Poets Society of America: "Francisco" (as "Route of the Conquerors")
Moria: "Spirit" and "Tchotchkes"
Movement: Our Bodies in Action, ed. Steve Carr (Sweetycat Press): "Flow"
New Verse News: "To Be, or to Be"
Solstice: A Magazine of Diverse Voices: "Nostalgia" (Finalist, 2019 Stephen Dunn Poetry Prize) and "Spin"
Spillway: "Sevens"

Publisher: Leah Huete de Maines
Editor: Christen Kincaid
Cover Art: *Veo, veo...* by Poli Marichal
Author Photo: Jaime Alvarez
Cover Design: Elizabeth Maines McCleavy

Order online: www.finishinglinepress.com
also available on amazon.com

Author inquiries and mail orders:
Finishing Line Press
PO Box 1626
Georgetown, Kentucky 40324
USA

Table of Contents

Nostalgia 1

Zen 2

Flow 3

Francisco 4

Spin 6

Cut 7

Russet 8

Raga 9

Spirit 10

Valentine 11

Voulez-Vous...? 12

To Be, or to Be 14

Hard C 15

Grave 16

Before 17

Transplant 19

Fire Season 2020 21

Sevens 23

Now, Somehow 24

Tchotchkes 25

Desire 27

For Jaime

Nostalgia

Like I'm waiting for kismet. *Maktoub.*
Waiting for a number, a letter—cryptic
for stage, grade. How many nodes did she
twist away? How many, how many... Tell me
to focus on healing. Friends bring guavas,
mini pumpkins, t-shirts, pens, soup. The house
is a garden: five white orchids, purple tulips,
yellow roses, irises. Red bromeliad clings
to bark, shape of a seahorse, air plants cresting
on two heads. Rearrangement happening
in cachepots. Rearrangement of a colon, color
of geranium in a Casbah courtyard. Animal
on hooks in back rooms of butcher shops
where my grandfathers blessed meat. How
did she swing my transverse meat around
to greet my small intestine, my distal ileum?
I wanted to catch the now-missing slice as it
slipped through her slick incision above my
navel. To feel the surgeon's finesse navigate
inside me, caress my organs, then choke
the cecum, the appendix to death. How
will the new partners jibe? How will they
groove with no past in such diminished
time? No memory of all the little madeleines
and Sunday's flow of hours. Slippery
fingertips straining to hold onto a waltz.

Zen

A man's tying his mask in the car next to mine.
A two-stringed mask. Gentleness. As if
he's protecting a child. Tying her sunhat. Child
lost in the wonder of tying her shoelaces. I'll never
know the man's face. Inside the market no smile
will be known. Eyes. You have to watch the eyes.
Some cold-shoulder. Some meet you head on,
invite. A wink. A crinkle. A glow. *Ojo* to *Ojo*.
A stare. Like decoding incunabula, reading a palm.
One set of strings has become the first bow.
The man's mask is not like one that was once
a blue yarmulke I found in a pocket—"Elise
and Joel" engraved on the satin in gold. A second
bow has just appeared. No more loose ends.

Flow

You wear the chemo home. It's in a fanny pack.
A pump's inside—attached to a port that's hooked
to a vein. No plunging necklines if you're vain.
If you unstrap straps, remember—you're connected.

You wear the pump for 46 hours. Every 12 days.
Know where your batteries are. You may need spares.
If you set the pack on a chair, don't dare walk far.
If the battery dies, know how to restart the flow,

or you'll panic, scream, fumble with buttons of fate.
Before your take-out mix, they'll infuse another brew.
If the pump beeps at 3AM, don't run around crazed.
You're yoked at the jugular for almost 2 days.

In the lab, cool nurses watch over you for 2 hours or 3.
Apple juice, jello, fruit cocktail, Lorna Doones.
When you're chained to the pack, it's a bitch to sleep.
You can lay the load beside you on the bed, or keep

it strapped. Energy bars, fruit juice, Lorna Doones.
Keep your fingers warm. No gelatos, fancy sorbets.
Lay the pack beside you at night. Or keep it strapped.
Don't die for sushi. No raw fish for a bit. Be brave.

No fingers in the fridge. No Sex on the Beach, mango
sorbets. You wear the chemo home. It's in a fanny pack.
Don't die for sushi. Think Shabu Shabu, teriyaki,
instead. No plunging necklines if you're vain.

Francisco

stands at the door of Schopería Iberia,
red tablecloths tempting, pillar of red

napkin rising up from a single wine glass
at each table, *no hay almohada tan suave*

como la conciencia tranquila written
on a chalk board—no pillow so soft

as a clear conscience—Francisco having
chosen the proverb, perhaps, though not

the menu, which today, market day, includes
sopa de vacuno, which I forget the meaning of,

and he says, as naturally as I would say,
"beef soup," and smiles, says he's Canadian,

been back in Chile seven years, and that his dad
was French-Canadian, his mother Chilean,

and I tell him I teach French, so he says:
"Call me François," as he seats us at a table

next to where he will sit with the chef, his
mother's sister, and we order *sopa de vacuno*

that comes, like every other soup in Chile,
with potato, yellow squash, a chunk of corn,

and a cilantro salsa called *pebre*, while
chickens sizzle on a spit—*pollos a la braza*—

specialty of Schopería Iberia here in Cauquenes,
small city along the Ruta de los Conquistadores

in this Maule region famous for carménères,
cabernets, and a tsunami eight years ago that

ravaged coastal towns thirty miles to the west
before Francisco returned to care for his mother

who died five days ago from skin cancer, and
I know he's been through hell, but I don't hold

him in my arms, just touch his arm as I slurp
sopa de vacuno, as other customers in this family-run

restaurant watch soccer on the big screen TV
this rainy day along the *Ruta de los Conquistadores*

where heavy mist obscures the hills beyond hay-
colored earth. And diners cheer a second goal.

Spin

I sit at a table dodging plates
as they whirl top speed around
a room. A plate twirler drops
wires on my head. My right hand
clenches emptiness when I
awake. A therapist friend asks
about the dream. I say first
cancer then surgery to excise
then chemo then infection then
transfusion then clot... Another
dream last night—our bathroom
un-renovated itself. Soap dish,
recessed in 1927 fern green tile,
excised over twenty years ago,
rebirthed along with the old
sink and toilet, beige shag rug
camouflaging original blue and
white cracked mosaic floor. Why
dream of earthquaked walls,
zigzagged ceiling? Dream of
plates spinning like a virus that
swirls around a neighborhood,
hooking even those who may
be #stillwaitingforGodot. Wild,
unhinged, loose-lipped virus
spouting droplets like delusions
we dodge with mask, glove,
separation. Lockdown. Unlock
the medals—voracious medals,
purple hearts. Pin them on
every soldier in this tragedy.
Hook them gently—oh ever so
gently—around the tenderness
of honor. Of gowns.

Cut
the day of the Christine Blasey Ford/Brett Kavanaugh hearing

He says he didn't do what she said he did.
Beef bouillon, Gatorade. Clear liquid diet.
Pre-colonoscopy jello, ginger ale. Brett
cries out: "Believe me! Oh, believe me!"
Method acting. He's Brando-ing. Trying out
Kowalski. Believe me, the doc can't writhe
his way through the mess. Quagmire along
the ascending route. The old boys will go to bat
for Brett. He'll climb, ease through. They'll go
for beer. Brett loves beer. Part of my colon
will go. No camouflage from the scope's *voir dire*.
One body has confessed, the facts laid bare.
One wins by skirting. *Huis clos* for my lining.
Suspicious divisions beneath both our wraps.

Russet
    for Jaime

He warms his hands to textured skin of cup,
a first embrace of morning. Rustic cup.
He threw it, swirled it into a jumbo cup
of porcelain, he glazed his earthy cup
a rugged russet shade, endowed the cup
with sturdy, curvy arm. Not round, his cup,
but oval-shaped—a spacious coffee cup.
His lips regale the thick-lipped rim of cup—
the only lips the rim permits to cup.
If ever he falls ill, his artsy cup
will take a break. A manufactured cup
of glass for chamomile or mint, no cup
to match the chemistry of homespun cup—
high fire flesh he'll ache to stroke, to cup.

Raga

There's no one sitting beside me. No one
in front. No one in back. There are no
rows, *no siddurim*—no prayer books—

stacked on tables in front of the sanctuary
doors this Day of Atonement. No eau de
parfum lingering between stained glass.

French roast the sole aroma. I'm listening
to a cantor on YouTube. Her voice is
nostalgia, it glistens, it's the end of drought,

our fires put out. It's a windfall of serenity,
pulse of astonishment. Now the rabbi's
perched on a boulder in mountains where

there is no fire. He's singing about the opening
of hearts. He's playing guitar. Over six feet
away is the cantor—this is a pre-recorded

portion. There's a bridge, a vigorous creek,
a waterfall. They're in casual clothes. Inside
the sanctuary they stand on either side

of the Ark in white *kittels*—a coincidental
distancing. The cantor smiles while she sings
words my father sang, his recitative rambling

through our house while he rehearsed, his
tremolos way too wavy for a child's patience.
His cantor's cap still lies inside my dresser

drawer, *kittel* given away long ago. Rocking
back and forth. I'm rocking back and forth
singing transliterated Hebrew on my screen.

Singing the English. I'm mesmerized by this
service: its relevance, compassion. Its panache.
Nothing is quite the same. Yet everything is.

Spirit
for Danielle

She had to move him to a home away from home.
A month went by, then lockdown came.
Alone in his room, only dreams could galavant.
The staff, they love his banter, his gentleness,

humanity. Two months went by, lockdown eased.
She visits now, she sits outside between the ferns
& birds of paradise. The staff, they love his jokes.
He sits inside, behind tall glass in the living room.

She sits outside amidst the potted palms & ferns.
They're talking on a cell. How she loves his calm,
his hair, that telltale grin behind the windowpane.
He tells her to be careful, not to trip, to lock

the doors at night. They're talking on their cells.
He's looking good though illness weakens him.
Once so robust! He tells her to lock the doors,
to not forget to use her Lancôme creams.

They FaceTime every day. He's looking good,
he's happy in the place, feels safer than before,
reminds her to smear her Lancôme creams.
Soon, she'll visit face-to-face in the patio,

six feet apart. He's happy in the place, feels safe.
He'll see her luminescent skin, she'll see his eyes
face-to-face between the ferns & birds of paradise.
Like vulnerable trees, their roots will intertwine—

no touch this time. He'll see her luminescence,
she'll see his eyes in this home away from home.
Like vulnerable trees, their roots will intertwine.
Together once more, dream unconfined.

Valentine

> *to my mother*

Your sister, then your nephew. Now me.
Glad you weren't here. You were spared.
"Got it all," said the doc. *Qué será*, will be.

Something to be said, you know, for heredity.
Forty-seven nodes excised. Seven impaired.
Your sister, then your nephew. Now me.

Four months of treatment, still another three.
Chemicals too harsh. Infections flared.
"Got it all," said the doc. *Qué será*, will be.

Ten days in a hospital bed. Transfusion spree.
Thirty pounds gained in a week. Fluid everywhere.
Your sister, then your nephew. Now me.

Ultrasounds, clots. Shots, scans. February
flick of blue print gowns. Code blue scare.
"Got it all," said the doc. *Qué será*, will be.

Missed the first Valencia orange on our tree,
first camellia. No Valentine's Day, *ma mère*.
Your sister, then your nephew. Now me.
"Got it all," said the doc. *Qué será*, will be.

Voulez-Vous...?

At least no broken bones when he fell out of our super high bed
Bought at the biggest Macy's one-day sale ever. Just a bloody

Cut on the neck from the French faux antique table hit on his way
Down to hardwood. Burrtec Waste picked up the box springs. What

Exertion lifting a sagging, sixteen-year-old Beautyrest onto its metal
Frame topped with plywood. Then we headed to another Macy's

Gargantuan bonanza to buy a mattress sans sag, sans box springs, sans
Highfalutin pillow top. We wondered about testing beds during Covid.

If we could lie on them, roll around on our tummy, side. Does virus
Jive on plastic? Tim, our sales associate, reassured we wouldn't be

Kissing death: They sanitize mattresses every evening. So we pushed our
Luck. While we were lounging, testing, another customer roamed by.

Making masked chitchat, I asked her if she wanted to join us atop our
Número Uno pick. I figured we would never recognize each

Other après-Covid. She declined the offer but left her Whole Foods
Purified water bottle on the ledge above our fave. Maybe it was some

Quirky talisman. Or maybe she wanted to make a swift getaway.
Regardless of her intentions, Tim was euphoric. Ours was his first

Sale since Macy's had reopened after a lockdown days before. I was
Thrilled for him despite the fortune we had just charged with zero interest

Until hell freezes over. Or at least for a year. My husband showed
Veritable relief he'd be asleep closer to the floor, didn't see me

Walk away from lucky Tim, lift my mask to take a sip from the woman's
X-water bottle thinking it was mine. Terror coursed through me.

You can imagine how much I was dying to Purell my mouth,
Zap any virus that could have seeped inside. We're still touching wood.

To Be, or to Be

Pale blue shirt against pale skin. Maroon
tie. Fauci looks tired as the anchor fires away.
He speaks about testing, transmissibility,
quarantines, and whatever else he must summon
up the vigor to explain, as the science flows
like the rain this morning, mud gushing down
the canyons where fires once roared. How many
times the doctor clarifies, like a Spanish teacher
must explain differences between *ser* and *estar*—
to be, or to be. Hundreds of repetitions
throughout a class, millions over a semester.
Like Fauci, the teacher maintaining patience,
calm, civility. The doctor is tired. Use *estar.*
Está cansado. Fauci is a cool dude. Use *ser.*

Hard C
for Dr. Daphne Stewart

Heels clicking on university linoleum
as we waited behind 1960s desks. Waited
for a chic *Parisienne* who spoke a language
we had hardly learned in high school. That
same pulse of hurried step—I hear it this
Wednesday afternoon from the examining
room. And every other Wednesday afternoon.
Same stiletto pump, dramatic entrée
into a room. The doctor exudes energy, like
Mademoiselle's hard Cs: her *cancan, cocorico,
coquette*. Daphne's twirling in her white coat
from patient to patient, always her treat of
chic underneath the rigor: flowery print, pleated
skirt, tailored dark gray sheath. Every day,
every week, this cascade of lexicon she has to
speak to the afflicted, as quickly as Mademoiselle.
Mellifluous, gentle flow of data as though chemo
were as absolute as the French subjunctive. As
though all you needed to survive was to
memorize expressions of desire, volition, doubt.
Fear. I fear her verdicts, her silence. Her second
sight. I want her to pronounce the *mot juste*
she never will. How can I hold onto her before she
disappears, before she swirls away from me,
rushes off to the next act of the same play. I want
to be chic again, wear black patent leather heels
like I wore to Mademoiselle's French Two. Drink
espresso for the very first time on Telegraph Avenue
in Berkeley. Hear the creek weave through campus.
I want to lie on the grass. Memorize past participles.

Grave
for Elaine

They'd bought a single plot for their two lives.
He said she'd go on the bottom, he'd go on top.
He thought for sure she'd be the first to die.

Their religion prescribes the depth of plot.
She paid extra to lie deeper inside the earth.
He said she'd go on the bottom, he'd go on top.

My parents rest near their spot. Six handbreaths
apart. Side by side for over twenty years.
She paid extra to lie deeper inside the earth.

Now divorce has come. She wants a single tier.
A tranquil place away from a freeway's drone.
My parents—side by side for over twenty years.

The single plot for two has sold; they'll lie alone.
Death's real estate's awarded them inflated sums.
She's bought a tranquil spot. No freeway drone.

Ocean breeze, thick morning mist before the sun.
They'd bought a single plot for their two lives.
Death's real estate's awarded them inflated sums.
He thought for sure she'd be the first to die.

Before
    for Elaine (1942-2022)

We'd take the La Brea Avenue bus to Hollywood,
walk Saturday afternoons up and down the Boulevard.

Lunch in a diner. Burgers, onion rings, fries. Root beers,
vanilla cokes. Your sweet sixteen at the Tick Tock

Restaurant on North Cahuenga. (A far cry from TikTok.)
Window shopping at Frederick's of Hollywood, Lerner's,

the Broadway Department Store. We carried no phone,
no credit cards. Just enough cash for the bus, lunch,

a pink or white lipstick at Newberry's five-and-dime.
Double date with your high school sweetheart—future

husband—at the Greek to hear Belafonte. You fixed me up
with Andy—he hardly spoke to me while we sat

up in the sky or waited after the show for Harry's autograph.
Your boyfriend's impatience on the rise. The program

still in my piano bench—Harry in a sexy orange calypso
shirt on the still shiny cover. A Studebaker or a two-tone

Chevy our wheels down Sunset Boulevard to Chautauqua
to the Pacific. Remember Brando in his red convertible

stopped at a red light next to us, Anna Kashfi next to Marlon?
We almost died right then & there. And then, & then,

we took the train to UC Berkeley. You lived in a dorm
while I got stuck in a rooming house whose roof caved in.

Later, you transferred to UCLA, got married, had a son, got
divorced. We drove to malls in the San Fernando Valley.

To Bullock's-turned-Macy's in Sherman Oaks—the tea room,
our favorite nesting place for laughter, tears, drama, analysis.

And endless cups of percolated coffee, all the while our wrists
dabbed with Madame Rochas' *Eau de Roche* from the duty-free

shop at Paris-Orly airport. Only our own diagnoses then. How
could we have imagined choices we'd have to make—

the shadows, the looming, the fear, the outcomes? And then,
and then, the Renaissance Faire. The dressing up, the hunt

for a young dulcimer player you liked were worth the long
drive. We'd walk around the Faire as years before we'd

walked in Hollywood—burgers & fries replaced by giant
turkey legs, corn on the cob. Root beers, cokes by overpriced

beer on tap. Clearer air in Agoura, slight ocean breeze.
Dreamy expedition releasing us from the quotidian. And

lunches at Factor's Famous Deli on Pico. And on the terrace
of the art museum, that time we watched Modigliani

move onto the second floor above Genghis Khan, bolts
of Amedeo's light gray carpet, his ferns, ficus, oversized

necks headed for the elevators. Always lunches. Always
devotion & conversation since the day we'd met in Dr. Gray's

tenth grade homeroom at a West Hollywood high school.
Always your telling me you were a day older than me. You,

Halloween babe, me, born on All Saints' Day, our birthdays
spanning the fiesta of *Día de los Muertos*. Always a day older.

Always first in death.

Transplant

There he was carrying a tray of bygone
at a San Francisco Hilton. Surrogate for

husband #1. Food services manager, not
engineer. Fluid English, not timid. I stared

at his name tag; he asked if I thought he
was Polish. I'd know the name anywhere.

That dramatic day I'd met the ex across
the bay at UC Berkeley—day of JFK's

assassination. The ex was carrying coffee
in one of those clunky white mugs. You know—

the ones my roomie would sometimes stuff
into her gigantic black purse she schlepped

from English to PolySci to Anthropology.
The surrogate's named Arezki. Algerian—like

the ex. Not Polish. I didn't know an immigration
lottery existed, but Arezki was one lucky

guy. I was in San Francisco for a transplant—
one lucky guy, my grandson, getting a kidney

from Mom. "It's like a birth," I told Arezki.
"Mother giving life a second time." "*Un miracle,*

une renaissance," he said, still carrying my
past. I knew our meal would be perfect,

like the English of husband #2. Transplant
to Tujunga from the Bronx. Same name—

Norman—as today's Maytag guy, one lucky
transplant from Moscow. There was Norman

carrying his black tool kit. Husband #2 carried
books with his name on covers and my name

in the acknowledgments. The repairman had
a tough job today: my Maytag needed a new

bearing. He told me, "You know, they put
Norman on my uniform. But I'm Armenian, my

name is Norayr. Hard to pronounce in English.
It means *new man*." I think about my grandson,

the precision of his surgery team, excision
of one organ, its rearrangement into the flesh

of a 24-year-old's tender body which will carry
the gift as long as it can. Today, this boy

shall replace his English name with *Norayr*:
One name shall be a surrogate for another.

Fire Season 2020

It kills me not to linger over tomato basil soup,
half a turkey sandwich with extra mayo, a mocha

at the mall. Though now we can dine *plein air*
in killer heat under a SoCal blanket of smoke-

choke air, mosquitoes attacking everywhere. Oh,
to roam *sans masque*—now *objet de dualité:*

shelter for pandemic then smoke. With so much
time on my hands, I should be writing a book.

I could write about Separation. Rage. Fear. About
mornings like this morning, lazing in bed, grilling

my brain about what went on yesterday, how I will
inhabit this day—mirror for mañana. Well after

mañana. Will I stand in line at Trader Joe's eyeing
amaryllis, narcissus, cacti lined up along the waiting

wall? Plants aching for touch. Fresh cut flowers
first thing you see upon gliding through the guarded

gate, red shopping cart handle moist under fearful
fingers. I could write about Zooms that friends have

maneuvered, take-out they've risked. Restaurant
parking lot canopies they've dined under—a *pis aller*

for solitude. Ennui. Dishwashing. And what about
doctors' office visits? Waiting rooms looking weird:

more spacious now, like purses. Chairs shoved up
against walls, stacked in closets, magazines exiled—

like lipsticks—along with coffee makers & creamer
& Sweet'N Low. And what about my husband—

his three-day, non-Covid hospital stay? I could write
about how hard he leaned on the passenger door

waiting for me, then on my arm to reach the ER door.
How he forgot I couldn't enter with him. How hard

he leaned on the nurse who led him away from me.
My sobbing in the car before heading home. How

bags of O+ blood began coursing through him—
urgently. Three bags of Separation. Rage. Fear.

Sevens

> *The Spelling Bee is a puzzle in the NYT*

To jigsaw seven letters into words—daily quest.
Seven days a week the Bee kept me awake.
For seven months of chemo, I obsessed.

Dry, watery, blurry eyes, yet I took the test.
Seven rankings for the Bee, like *amazing, great*.
To jigsaw seven letters into words—daily quest.

Until I reached *genius*—never a day's rest.
Family sprawled on the duvet for my sake.
We racked brains for seven months, obsessed,

stared at my iPhone, went for points, pressed
for pangrams, like *pockmark, garbanzo, clambake*.
To jigsaw seven letters into words—daily quest.

Fixation's gone now along with chemo's recess.
Should cancer recur, will the Bee retake,
or will Sudoku & nines help me to re-obsess?

My subscription's expiring. Quit or acquiesce?
How will renewal play on my ultimate fate?
To jigsaw seven letters into words—daily quest.
For seven months of chemo, I obsessed.

Now, Somehow

Feather at the bottom of the cage:
light grey with whiff of white. His
head dips to one side—eye meets plume.
He squawks. No appeasing the bird now.

Light grey with whiff of white, like
my eyebrows before. They're half-gone now.
He squawks, no appeasing him, like
when my eyelashes disappeared somehow.

Eyebrows—they are mostly gone now.
Bird dander drifting down the cage,
eyelashes slipping into my eyes somehow.
Hair floating all around the house.

Dander floating around the cage, the room.
Scant white threads clinging to my scalp,
somehow. Hair drifting around the house.
On hardwood, the inside of berets, caps.

Stark wiry threads hanging to my scalp.
I envy female anchors, stare at TV hair.
Hair on pillows, collars now, somehow.
Look at the geography of part, flip, wave.

Look at female anchors, stare at their hair.
Headbands camouflage the scant somehow.
Look at the rendezvous of brunette with dress.
Blue eye shadow masks no eyelashes now.

Scarves around my head conceal the scant.
Another feather at the bottom of the cage.
Eye shadow masking no eyelashes now. Bird—
restore me with your fallen plumes. Somehow.

Tchotchkes

I am no defector from the Moscow Circus,
but I'm praying for toilet tissue. Shelves
half-bare as I stand here stunned like when

Robin Williams stands in a coffee aisle
in the movie "Moscow on the Hudson,"
gobsmacked by American supermarket

plethora. Hasn't the coin flipped to the other
side? Now a stranger points to a bottom
shelf. "Don't buy that brand!" she warns me.

"It leaves little bits of tissue—there." She
points again. This scene just before lockdown,
masks, gloves, swabs... Before Sunday's

family birthday Zoom. I put on my Santa Fe
Indian Market turquoise earrings, removed
my sweats, put on a sundress. I was counting

on a chat with some I hadn't seen in a while.
I found loud music instead. Wild jumping,
bare baby bottom, diaper changing. A Costco

chocolate cake with twenty-one candles. Sure,
we sang, let them eat cake. I wish I could say
someone noticed my lip gloss or how long

my hair had grown since chemo ended last
year, my stark white hair piled on top of my
head, hair grown in thicker than before.

Or that my kitchen sparkled like the one
in MSNBC interviews. White, luminous
kitchen with a bowl of fruit arranged

on the counter—oranges and apples
replaced by apricots and nectarines as
the months have rolled by, and spring

has switched to summer. A white orchid
has morphed into a sunflower, and three
ceramic squirrels surround a stubby

cactus. Don't you love these intimate
settings despite the back story, tragedy
you can forget for a moment eyeing

the tchotchkes—the clay giraffes and
hippos, the seashells, Inuit bears, and
miniature ships—in between the combed

or unread tomes of the imagined or
unimaginable scripts? New oeuvres keep
slipping in next to the old—rhythmically,

naturally gliding in next to their own kind,
who shelter them, make them feel at home.
Who knows when their authors will

no longer have to sit or stand next to a lone
pineapple on a granite counter or a fiddle
leaf fig? Or a light mahogany baby grand.

Desire

pre-mask, post-lockdown

I put on mascara yesterday—
oh not to go to lunch or anywhere.
Forgot to wash it off last night.
Stain under my eyes this morning.
Wasn't there somewhere I'd gone?
Oh—a walk in the neighborhood.

I put on lipstick for the neighborhood—
Berry Kiss. Put on earrings, too, yesterday.
Lapiz lazul teardrops. Silver from Santiago.
More earrings ache for action somewhere:
hoops, spirals in boxes, dressers, mourning.
I put on sunblock. Didn't wash it off at night.

I dreamt *très tropiques*. Sexy Tahitian night.
King palms slow dancing in the neighborhood,
dropping fronds all over lawns till morning.
They'll stay a week. Trash picked up yesterday.
Still on the job, workers risking everywhere.
Some clocking off intact, some a no-go.

The San Gabriels sparkle. Pollution's gone.
Cars paralyzed in driveways day and night.
I put on leggings to meet no one anywhere:
red hearts walk alone in the neighborhood.
Even a peacock kept his distance yesterday,
turquoise breezy in the truce of morning.

Mourning doves on the wire hang all morning.
They're plotting rendezvous, cool places to go.
Bulbuls chirp. Do they remember yesterdays?
Three babies slept in the orange tree last night.
I put on a dreamcatcher to walk the neighborhood—
put on hope to transport me fast, elsewhere,

take me to a past when I could go anywhere.
No hummingbird lockdown this morning.
No feeders shuttered in the neighborhood.
Camellias blooming, azalea petals not yet gone.
Our first cactus orchid may burst open tonight
along with champagne chilling since yesterday.

I'm putting on a little black dress to go nowhere.
Just you and me, darling, *ce soir* in the neighborhood.
Let's sip till morn. Put on yesterday's refrains.

Judith Terzi is the author of *Museum of Rearranged Objects* (Kelsay Books) and five previous chapbooks including *Casbah* and *If You Spot Your Brother Floating By* (Kattywompus Press), and *Ghazal for a Chambermaid* and *Sharing Tabouli* (Finishing Line). Her poems appear widely in literary journals and anthologies including the *Atlanta Review, The Examined Life Journal, Fire and Rain: Ecopoetry of California, Lunch Ticket, MacQueen's Quinterly, Moria, The New Verse News, Solstice, Spillway,* and *Times They Were A-Changing: Women Remember the 60s & 70s*. BBC/Radio 3 featured her poem "Ode to Malala Yousafzai" in the "Heroines" episode of *Words and Music*. "Nostalgia," in this collection, was a finalist for the 2019 Stephen Dunn Poetry Prize. She holds an M.A. in French Language and Literature and taught high school French in Pasadena, California, as well as English at California State University, Los Angeles and in Algiers, Algeria. Living with a soccer fanatic from Chile, she knows more about soccer than you'd suspect.

www.ingramcontent.com/pod-product-compliance
Lightning Source LLC
LaVergne TN
LVHW041512070426
835507LV00012B/1526